The Beauty
of *Love*

The Beauty of Love

Deborah Reeves

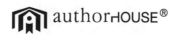

AuthorHouse™ LLC
1663 Liberty Drive
Bloomington, IN 47403
www.authorhouse.com
Phone: 1-800-839-8640

Published by AuthorHouse 02/22/2014

ISBN: 978-1-4918-6438-8 (sc)
ISBN: 978-1-4918-6437-1 (e)

Library of Congress Control Number: 2014902990

Any people depicted in stock imagery provided by Thinkstock are models, and such images are being used for illustrative purposes only. Certain stock imagery © Thinkstock.

This book is printed on acid-free paper.

Because of the dynamic nature of the Internet, any web addresses or links contained in this book may have changed since publication and may no longer be valid. The views expressed in this work are solely those of the author and do not necessarily reflect the views of the publisher, and the publisher hereby disclaims any responsibility for them.

Scripture quotations marked KJV are from the Holy Bible, King James Version (Authorized Version). First published in 1611. Quoted from the KJV Classic Reference Bible, Copyright © 1983 by The Zondervan Corporation.

TABLE OF CONTENTS

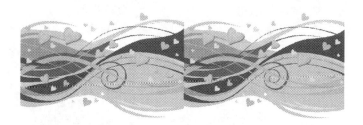

Thanks to my dear Sisters and Friends

Katherine Stapleton, a sister in Christ, was a blessing to me in helping me title this book. I thank you, sister, for the love you share. May your life be filled with love daily. I also want to thank my faithful friend and sister in Christ, Donna Brown. She continues to be a blessing by editing the books for me. She has been blessed with a loving kind heart. I pray that she continues to allow God to use her for his glory.

Loving Thanks

I am so thankful to my daughter, Cecelia Reeves-Chavez, who was my primary editor. She also designed the cover of this book. She has been and continues to be a beacon of love with a positive disposition. I want to give a special thanks to my nephew, Timothy Short, who provided the three landscape illustrations. He is very talented and is a student at Georgia State University.

With Loving Gratitude

To my husband, Julian Reeves, a special man in so many ways, I thank God for you. Thank you for your support in everything I do.

FOREWORD

We have a unique need unlike all the other creatures created by a loving God. We are created in God's image, infused with a deep desire within our souls to love and to be loved. Those who have this great desire to be Christ-like and be clothed in the same manner with the virtue of love strive to be recognized as loving and caring.

Deborah Reeves, a faithful servant of God, has made love her center of interest and draws our attention to The Beauty of Love, a book of inspirational poems to help us take meaningful steps toward a better life. We have the power to change our life by changing ourselves.

By reading these songlike expressions of love, one should develop a better appreciation for Jesus and His love for us. The biggest challenge in life is to learn to love, to understand love, and have compassion towards all men. Across the ages, men in different endeavors have expressed their thoughts on love. Shakespeare eloquently beatified love with his quill by penning, "By heaven, I do love, and it hath taught me to rhyme, and to be melancholy." Songwriters and poets have articulated their opinions with quaint expressions such as,"marriage is more than the entanglement of two hearts; it is the entwining of two lives, forever." But Jesus has said it best in John 15:13, "Greater love has no man than this, than to lay down one's life for his friends." This is the foundation of her book of poetry. Reeves draws effectively from her Christian background, church involvement, and a keen awareness of sacrificial love.

Who should read this book? Everybody! Two young hearts experiencing new adventures of love, every moment they spend together, need godly guidance. The casual reader who wants a life of joy, his inner voice will be reminded of God's law and how He gives life abundantly. Christians who want to be like Christ in all areas of their life and service will benefit from these poetic writings. Reeves has addressed topics such as belief in God, getting to know God, and knowing self. Her insights of life are meant to gently guide the reader through scriptural examples which have the power to change our lives.

As Ministering Evangelist of the church of Christ at Mount Vernon, I would like to thank my sister in Christ for this wonderful gift to the world. Reeves' treatises on love remind me of the everlasting power of love. I am encouraged and acknowledge that the Christian virtue of love is eternal. 1 Corinthians 13:13, "And now abide faith, hope, love, these three; but the greatest of these *is* love." Deborah Reeves' writings have enriched my life and I know this book will enrich yours.

Anthony Spradley

It Is Time

It is time to love, time to pray, time to let go, and time to make peace. It is time for hope, time for joy, time to forgive, time to surrender. It is time for grace, time for patience, time to transcend the evil state of being. It is time for life. It is time that is available to us now to move in the right direction. It is time to call on the Lord and live in his presence. It is time to bring joy and happiness to someone else's life. It is time that we make peace and forgive ourselves. It is time. So do it, and free yourself from all the pent-up hurt, guilt, and hate. Move forward, move now, and move righteously.

"To everything there is a season, and a time to every purpose under the heaven: A time to be born, and a time to die; a time to plant, and a time to pluck up that which is planted; A time to kill, and a time to heal; a time to break down, and a time to build up . . ."
Ecclesiastes 3:1-3

Let Me In

I want to be there for you. I want to be able to support you in ways that no one else can or should. I want to love you with love so fulfilling that your life is transformed into a life of bliss. It is up to you to allow me in, to open your heart and let the rich flow pump through your veins. You can feel more alive than you ever have. Life is so much more than you have freed yourself to embrace. Stop standing in your own way. Give yourself a chance to experience the full throttle of life. Welcome me in.

"Nor height, nor depth, nor any other creature, shall be able to separate us from the love of God, which is in Christ Jesus our Lord." Romans 8:39

Open Up Your Heart

A heart is a precious thing. Out of it may flow hope, love, and peace. It may bring a smile to the wounded; sing songs to the weary. Opening your heart will let you experience the feelings of happiness and bliss more than you ever have or thought you could have. An open heart can open other doors which were closed to you before. The warmth, healing, and relief you will have will be unbelievable. Your eyes will be opened to a new world, a new dream, and a new life. Open your heart to God today. God will show you just how beautiful you are when you walk for his word.

"O ye Corinthians, our mouth is open unto you, our heart is enlarged."
II Corinthians 6:11

Ready

It is time to get ready for life. It is time to enjoy the life that we have. It is time to take courage and believe that the abundant living is for you. It is time to stop hiding from life and from the great blessings in store for you. Get ready, be ready, and stay ready to live in the here and now. God has put you here right now for a reason. Pray and stay in prayer being obedient to his word and you will understand how God has prepared you to be ready.

"But of that day and that hour knoweth no man, no, not the angels which are in heaven, neither the Son, but the Father. Take ye heed, watch and pray: for ye know not when the time is." Mark 13:32-33

When Things Happen

When things happen, you can love. When things happen, you can keep smiling. When things happen, dream of what you want to happen. When things happen you can make the best or the worst of it. When things happen, you can ask God to direct your mouth, thoughts, and heart to do the right thing. When things happen, take courage and do not conform to this world. When things happen, go forward doing good for God.

"And be not conformed to this world: but be ye transformed by the renewing of your mind, that ye may prove what is that good, and acceptable, and perfect, will of God. For I say, through the grace given unto me, to every man that is among you, not to think of himself more highly than he ought to think; but to think soberly, according as God hath dealt to every man the measure of faith." Romans 12:2-3

Let It Go

Life is filled with so much suffering that it is hard to get from one place to another and realize what you have actually experienced. Sometimes, life looks like a jungle. Sometimes, it feels like we have been catapulted into a massive web of confusion. There are times when we are not easily able to get where we want to go or do not feel able to weed through the plethora of decisions we could make. There are times when all seems to press against us and we are not moving forward as we think. I ask you this question, are you trying to take on too much in your life? Do you think you are in control? Are you trying to conquer life, or are you holding on to too much stuff? Let it go, and free yourself of being the super person you perceive yourself to be. Let it go, and allow God to move you and direct your steps. You are not in control.

"O Lord, I know that the way of man is not in himself: it is not in man that walketh to direct his steps. O Lord, correct me, but with judgment; not in thine anger, lest thou bring me to nothing." Jeremiah 10:23-24

Let Me

Let me take the time to say thanks. Let me share with you just how important you are to me. Let me explain the blessings you have brought into my life. Let me know that you are present in the moment. Let me be a blessing to you. You have made a positive difference in my life. There have been tears and hurt; but, there have also been joy, love, and hope in my life. Let me be the one in your life who helps you to see God in you. Let me celebrate life with you as we glorify God.

"Neither do men light a candle, and put it under a bushel, but on a candlestick; and it giveth light unto all that are in the house. Let your light so shine before men, that they may see your good works, and glorify your Father which is in heaven." Matthew 5:15-16

Thank You, God

Thank you, God, for your love and blessings you freely give to me daily. You have been and are always with me. You have always provided me with what I need and my heart's desires. I pray that you bless me to hold on to your love and your commandments. Bless me to be a blessing to others. Help me, God, to be a support and a positive force in my family, my worship place, my workplace, my community, and wherever you send me. Let me shine for you each day.

"First, I thank my God through Jesus Christ for you all, that your faith is spoken of throughout the whole world. For God is my witness, whom I serve with my spirit in the gospel of his Son, that without ceasing I make mention of you always in my prayers; . . . ." Romans 1:8-9

You Know Best

I trust in all you have done for me and continue to do for me. I thank you for knowing and taking care of my best needs. I pray that I am obedient to you in all things. I know that you know best in all things. I know that I should always allow your blessings, power, and commandments to live in my heart and bloom in my actions. You know what is best for me today and every day. I pray that I surrender my heart and will to you daily, because you know how to provide the best in the worst situation. Thank you for being my Father who knows best.

"But the father said to his servants, Bring forth the best robe, and put it on him; and put a ring on his hand, and shoes on his feet: And bring hither the fatted calf, and kill it; and let us eat, and be merry: . . . ." Luke 15:22-23

The Lord Will Deliver

I thank you, God, for your deliverance. Please prepare me for a better place. Please allow me to hold to your unchanging hands in this changing world. You know my walk. You know my faith. You know how others see me. Bless me daily to be who you want me to be daily. Let me do the work that you created me to do for you. Let me shine for Jesus as a brilliant jewel unblemished by the trappings of this world. I know that if I trust in you, obey your word, and walk by faith, you will deliver me. Let me be delivered from the trappings of this world and of my own mind. Let me be willing to be delivered by you and fully live a life of abundance.

"Go and cry unto the gods which ye have chosen; let them deliver you in the time of your tribulation. And the children of Israel said unto the LORD, We have sinned: do thou unto us whatsoever seemeth good unto thee; deliver us only, we pray thee, this day." Judges 10:14-16

I Need Help

Dear Lord, help me where I need help. Help me to know that you will never leave me alone. Help me to be free to be me. Help me, Lord. I need you more than I am able to express with words. I cannot take on the world. I cannot live without you. I need help, Lord, each and every day. I need help with my thoughts, my heart, my words, my actions, and my direction. I know that you have the help I need in all things. I know that you have helped me in past times. I need help in being deliberate in bringing my needs to you.

"And Asa cried unto the LORD his God, and said, LORD, it is nothing with thee to help, whether with many, or with them that have no power: help us, O LORD our God; for we rest on thee, and in thy name we go against this multitude. O LORD, thou art our God; let no man prevail against thee."
2 Chronicles 14:11

Instrument of Peace

May I be able to see peace in the things I do. May
I have the spirit which seeks righteousness. May
I move forward with the gentleness of God's love.
May I look for the peace in others. God, help me
to serve you through Jesus in the right way. God,
help me not to cause problems for myself and
others by holding back or stuffing things within.
Lord, help me to take courage, be strong, and be
a good steward of what you have given me to use
here on earth. Lord, help me to be an instrument
of peace by the way I talk, think, and live.

"He shall enter into peace: they shall rest in their beds, each one walking
in his uprightness." Isaiah 57:2

I Can Do

I can do all things with the help of the Lord. I can
walk through darkness, jungles, and the deepest
caves and know that God will be ever present. I
can run on dry, hard, wet or muddy paths and not
stumble as I traverse the course. I can fly above
the sky, the world, the intellect of man and abound
in God's grace because I can do all things through
Christ who strengthens me. I can do all these things
if I follow Christ, not because of selfish ambitions.

"Not that I speak in respect of want: for I have learned, in whatsoever
state I am, therewith to be content. I know both how to be abased, and I
know how to abound: everywhere and in all things I am instructed both
to be full and to be hungry, both to abound and to suffer need. I can do
all things through Christ which strengtheneth me." Philippians 4:11-13

Take Heart

Take heart and go forward, know that the Lord is good and that he provides us with all that we need. Take heart and see that through the glory of God, he will take care of all things regarding life and godliness. God will give us what we need, when we need it, if we trust and obey his commandments. God even tells us in Proverbs that he will give us the desires of our heart. "Delight thyself also in the LORD: and he shall give thee the desires of thine heart," Psalm 37:4. What is in your heart? Let your heart be rejuvenated in love. Take heart and smile, know that God loves you. God wants the best for you. What do you want for yourself? Thank God and love Christ daily. See what a blessing you can be for the Lord. You can take heart if your heart is pure.

"The king shall joy in thy strength, O Lord; and in thy salvation how greatly shall he rejoice! Thou hast given him his heart's desire, and hast not withholden the request of his lips. Selah. For thou preventest him with the blessings of goodness: thou settest a crown of pure gold on his head." Psalm 21:1-3

Although

Although I walk through the shadow of death, I am not afraid, because I know that my God is with me. God is with me and has not left me alone, even when I experience days that seem to turn into nightmares. I will trust in God to direct my path. Although it may seem that the world is against me, I stand tall in the Lord. Although my eyes grow full of tears, I know that I am not alone. I know God is with me no matter how many adverse experiences I have. Although I will feel pain and sorrow, I know that it does not compare with the sacrifice Christ made for me and you.

"The Lord is my shepherd; I shall not want. He maketh me to lie down in green pastures: he leadeth me beside the still waters. He restoreth my soul: he leadeth me in the paths of righteousness for his name's sake. Yea, though I walk through the valley of the shadow of death, I will fear no evil: for thou art with me; thy rod and thy staff they comfort me. Thou preparest a table before me in the presence of mine enemies: thou anointest my head with oil; my cup runneth over. Surely goodness and mercy shall follow me all the days of my life: and I will dwell in the house of the Lord forever." Psalm 23

May the Lord

May the Lord bless you to do well today. May He give you the joys of the heart and allow you the pleasure of many blessings. May the Lord grant you the peace of mind and the courage of heart to stand up for what is right. May the Lord give you the strength to pray for more strength daily as you go through the different challenges of life. Trust in God and follow his directions to lead your life. Be sure-footed in the word. Build your house upon the Rock. Have a firm foundation. Be immovable and full of faith. Be of good cheer; know that God has a plan for you. Thank him and be grateful for what he is doing for you now.

"When thou cuttest down thine harvest in thy field, and hast forgot a sheaf in the field, thou shalt not go again to fetch it: it shall be for the stranger, for the fatherless, and for the widow: that the LORD thy God may bless thee in all the work of thine hands." Deuteronomy 24:19

"That thy trust may be in the LORD, I have made known to thee this day, even to thee." Proverbs 22:19

There Is A Time

There is a time for joy and pain. There is a place
of smiles and sadness. There is an opportunity
for wonder and fear. There is a time for hope and
faith. There is a time to be lifted and a time to lift
another. There is a time for receiving and a time
for giving. There is a time to be busy and a time
to be still. There is a time to speak up and a time
to be silent. No matter what time it is, it is always
time to seek God and serve him. The time is now.

"I said in mine heart, God shall judge the righteous and the wicked:
for there is a time there for every purpose and for every work."
Ecclesiastes 3:17

Lord, Lift Me Up

Lord, carry me through the dark channels in my life.
Lord, give me hope, joy, and peace in the face of
adversity. Lord, bring forth your goodness and mercy
upon me as I serve you here on earth. God, help me to
be the child you would have me to be. Lord, you know
just how much I struggle within myself to be a good
daughter. Lord, you know, in my heart, how I wanted
to be the best daughter I could be to my mother,
father, and grandparents. Lord, you know I tried to be
an encouragement and a blessing. Thank you, Lord,
for the prayers we shared. Lord, you know that I am
thankful for the time you gave us together. I thank you,
Lord, for the voice to sing songs of precious memories
of your love to mom, dad, and grandparents. I thank
you, God, for lifting me up when I am down. I ask you,
God, to lift me up as I lift another up in glorifying you.

"And that bringeth me forth from mine enemies: thou also hast lifted
me up on high above them that rose up against me: thou hast delivered
me from the violent man." 2 Samuel 22:49

I Know My God

I know that my God is alive and he hears my prayers. I know that God will use me to do his good works. I know that God keeps his promises. I know that God is long-suffering to me. I know that God is always there for me and he knows my heart. God is an awesome God and he provides blessings and guidance to all his children. Stand up. Stand tall on faith and God's word. I know my God is a loving God who wants all to come to him in obedience. God does not want any of us to perish. He wants everyone to be saved. I know he wants you. Come to him now.

"The Lord is not slack concerning his promise, as some men count slackness; but is longsuffering to us-ward, not willing that any should perish, but that all should come to repentance." 2 Peter 3:9

Wake Up

It is time to wake up from sleep and thank God for blessing you. It is time for love, joy, peace, and faith to rule your life. Tomorrow is not promised to us, nor will today wait for us to start living. Be sober-minded and go forth with the vigor and the energy Christ has blessed you with today. Wake up and do not throw your life away worrying about the things of this world. Do not be afraid of the world or the people in it. Do not sleep-walk your life away. The things of the world are temporary. Wake up now and live the life you have.

"Therefore let us not sleep, as do others; but let us watch and be sober."
1 Thessalonians 5:6

Let Not

Let not your heart be troubled, let God fill in
the emptiness of your life. Let not your life be
diminished by avoiding, hiding, fear, or shame. Let
not your fear keep you from your blessings. Let
not your thoughts be of evil and hate. Let not your
energy be spent returning wrongs done to you. Let
not others persuade you to do wrong, but let God
into your life. Allow God to lead you in a fruitful,
successful, profitable life of love, forgiveness,
and thanksgiving. God will see you through more
than you can ever imagine or expect. Yes, God
is real, and all things are possible with God.

"Let not your heart be troubled: ye believe in God, believe also in me."
John 14:1

"But Jesus beheld them, and said unto them, With men this is impossible;
but with God all things are possible." Matthew 19:26

The Blessings

My God has created in me and you a blessing.
This blessing brings forth clarity of heart and
allows life to be seen from a pure perspective.
It brings forth renewal, restoration, and revival.
It lightens the heart and allows us to breathe
smoothly, deeply and brings a sigh of relief from
all the things that were weighing us down. I will
exhale and allow God's blessings to permeate
my life. What will you do? The blessing should
not be taken for granted but valued. I will share
the blessing with others. What will you do? Be
blessed and accept the blessings God has for you.

"The blessings of thy father have prevailed above the blessings of my
progenitors unto the utmost bound of the everlasting hills: they shall be
on the head of Joseph, and on the crown of the head of him that was
separate from his brethren." Genesis 49:26

It Is Hard

Why is it hard to say I love you, I forgive you, and I am sorry? Why do I have to ask for words? Is it hard to love me? Is it hard to say forgive me? Is it hard to say I am sorry? Do you want to love? Are you ready to forgive? Do you want to be forgiven? Are you afraid to love? Are you questioning whether you deserve love or forgiveness? Is it hard because you are afraid that if you say it out loud, will you be taken advantage of? Is it hard because you have not experienced love or forgiveness in your youth? Why do you think it continues to be hard for you?

"And forgive us our sins; for we also forgive every one that is indebted to us. And lead us not into temptation; but deliver us from evil." Luke 11:4

"In this the children of God are manifest, and the children of the devil: whosoever doeth not righteousness is not of God, neither he that loveth not his brother." I John 3:10

"And the disciples were astonished at his words. But Jesus answereth again, and saith unto them, Children, how hard is it for them that trust in riches to enter into the kingdom of God!" Mark 10:24

As I

As I let go, I free myself of all the constraints I have held onto. As I let go, I can feel the warmth and pleasure of the blessings God so richly gives; I don't have to shoulder life by myself. As I let go, I can see the light, and it gets clearer as I let my problems fall by the wayside. As I let go, I like myself a lot better, because I can see myself a lot better. I can see the gentleness, kindness, love, hope, and joy with God which he has blessed me with. These attributes and virtues were available to me all the time; however, I could not see them. I lacked the space for them to reside or to reveal themselves. In order for me to receive more of God's blessings in my life, there has to be less of me and more of Him. As I free myself of me, I can and will receive more of Him as I immerse myself in His word and work. Now God's attributes and virtues can grow and multiply in me as I become fertile ground for Him.

"He must increase, but I must decrease. He that cometh from above is above all: he that is of the earth is earthly, and speaketh of the earth: he that cometh from heaven is above all." John 3:30-31

God Grant Me

God, grant me the ability and desire to receive your love that you have for me. God gives me blessings that I can be of good service to Him. He loves me greatly. He holds me close and helps me through the difficulties in my life. God, grant me the peace that will calm my soul and mind. God, make me into who you want me to be this day. God, grant me the power to forget about self and sanctify and worship you by the way that I live each day. God, grant me the understanding that I am here to do your service, not my own.

"Then Eli answered and said, Go in peace: and the God of Israel grant thee thy petition that thou hast asked of him." 1 Samuel 1:17

Help Me To Take Time

Lord, help me to take time to see you in ways that I have not been open to before. Help me, Lord, to know that you are in control today, yesterday, and forever. Help me to take the time to understand your word and know that there is no other power or strength that is greater. Help me to take the time and breathe you in. You are the breath of life. Help me to take time to release myself of the deception of this world, the temporary material things and positions which can project the illusion of greatness. Help me to take the time to see how I may allow things to block my blessings, or to hold me back from receiving the joy and peace you have for me to receive right now. I thank you, Lord, for helping me to take time in prayer and study of your word. Help me to take time to apply your word as my guiding light each day.

"Let thine hand help me; for I have chosen thy precepts." Psalm 119:173

"Be pleased, O Lord, to deliver me: O Lord, make haste to help me." Psalm 40:13

"Help me, O Lord my God: O save me according to thy mercy:.. ." Psalm 109:26

"Let my soul live, and it shall praise thee; and let thy judgments help me." Psalm 119:175

Thank You For Today

Today, I am looking for the good in me and in others. I will pray. I will let God direct my steps. I will stand still and wait on the Lord. Thank You for today and all the blessings you have given me. I am giving thanks for what I have right now. Thank you for the good things, hard things, joyful things, and bad things in my life. Thank you for today, God. Today is what you have given me; I will live in this moment in this day. I will take what you give and use it to bless my life and the life of others. Thank you for today.

"For Moses had said, Consecrate yourselves today to the LORD, even every man upon his son, and upon his brother; that he may bestow upon you a blessing this day." Exodus 32:29

Lord I Know You

Lord, I know that you are present in my life. I know you cared for me before I was born. I know you care and that you have a plan for me. Lord, I know you will put me in the right place at the right time to show your marvelous work and power in my life. I know, Lord, how great you are. You are magnificent. I know Lord, how powerful you are. Help me to keep going when I am down. Help me to be humble when I am successful. Help me to believe when believing seems unreal. Help me to know that nothing is impossible with you as my leader. Help me to love my family and others when they seem very unlovable. Help me to go on when the going is rough. Lord, help me to never give up. Help me to never give in to evil. Help me to allow myself to be helped by you.

"I know thy works, and where thou dwellest, even where Satan's seat is: and thou holdest fast my name, and hast not denied my faith, even in those days wherein Antipas was my faithful martyr, who was slain among you, where Satan dwelleth." Revelation 2:13

The Way

The way is not always clear, nor is the path always smooth, but keep going. The light is not always apparent in the beginning of a dark cavern; keep going. Remember, life does not owe you anything. What we get is a blessing, and it is good to give thanks. The way to God is the way that will build our spirit, fill us with truth, and build our faith if we follow God's way. Ask, seek, knock (ASK) daily and keep going. Remember to ask. The way is narrow which leads unto life, and few will find it. Broad is the way that leads to destruction and many will go in that way. Which way will you choose?

"Jesus saith unto him, I am the way, the truth, and the life: no man cometh unto the Father, but by me." John 14:6

Thank You

Thank you, Lord, for putting me in this place, in this environment, and in this spirit in this time in my life. I could have been in a lot of other places, places that are not so conducive to my needs or desires. I thank God for knowing what is best for me and moving me in the right direction. Thank you, God, for the growth you have given me to know that my past is not my future. Bless me to understand that I cannot attribute the blessings you allowed to flow through me to be credited to my greatness, but yours. Help me as I continue to travel through life to put all my faith, hope, and thought in you, in Jesus' name I thank you.

"In every thing give thanks: for this is the will of God in Christ Jesus concerning you." 1 Thessalonians 5:18

You Know Me

You know me and what you made me to do. You know me and how I can better know myself. You know me because I was made in your image. You know my heart, my soul, my spirit. You know my hopes, anxieties, and dreams. You know what I need and don't need. Let me not be deceived by idols but to hold on to what is best for me. You know that when I follow you, the world will not be my friend, and that is all right. Let me be willing to follow you. You know that I need to be led by your guidance daily. You know what you have planned for my life. Help me to know you better as I live this life.

"If the world hate you, ye know that it hated me before it hated you."
John 15:18

Let Me Love You

Let me love you now. Don't put love off until later. Don't wait for a more convenient time to love and to be loved. Why wait for love when you can receive it and give it right now? Why run away from love? Where are you running to? What do you hope to gain by putting love last? You can experience a soaring of bliss and elation. If you let me love you, you can receive the blessings and peace that love brings. Don't be afraid to be loved. Don't think that you are not worth loving. Love is powerful. Love is strong. Love will strengthen you. Love is of God. God is love. Be of God.

"And as he reasoned of righteousness, temperance, and judgment to come, Felix trembled, and answered, Go thy way for this time; when I have a convenient season, I will call for thee." Acts 24:25

"He that loveth not knoweth not God; for God is love." 1 John 4:8

Let Not

Let not your heart be troubled or your spirit be down. Why do we worry about things in life? Why do we allow things to determine our peace of mind? Let not your feelings be your guide of how you live, let God be your guide. Let not your behavior be of selfishness; but full of love for God, your fellow man, and self. Put your faith in God and receive his grace. Let not a bitter word neither come from your mouth nor enter your heart. Let not your joy and love fade by the things that happen to you in this world, but grow in faith and wisdom as you seek God through all things.

"Let not your heart be troubled: ye believe in God, believe also in me. In my Father's house are many mansions: if it were not so, I would have told you. I go to prepare a place for you." John 14:1-2

Not To Know

What are you pretending not to know? There are things we choose to be blind to. There are things that are not as we see them and we know it. There are people who are different from what we assess them to be. We make assessments of others based on our insecurities. We can see something in someone that causes us discomfort. The discomfort is due to a feeling of inadequacy we have of ourselves. We project that feeling onto others. We choose not to know that our discomfort is because of how deficient we feel about ourselves. If we take the time to really examine ourselves and be honest, we might not like what we see. There are things, people, and situations that would serve us better if we were present in the moment and honest with ourselves. What is it that you are choosing not to know about yourself? Take the time to know God so that you may know yourself better and make the changes that are needed to have a better life.

"For I determined not to know any thing among you, save Jesus Christ, and him crucified." 1 Corinthians 2:2

"Know ye not, that to whom ye yield yourselves servants to obey, his servants ye are to whom ye obey; whether of sin unto death, or of obedience unto righteousness?" Romans 6:16

Let It Be

Oh Lord, bless me where I am, and let it be a blessing for you today. Let me be the one you would have me to be to serve you today. Hold me close and help me through dark days. God, give me strength to stand tall and firm in truth and love as a faithful servant. Let it be me. Let it be me who cares for others, visits the sick, helps the homeless, prays for my enemies, calls the lonely people, smiles at strangers, says a kind word to those in pain and loves those who seem unlovable. Let it be me you use today.

"Now therefore come thou, let us make a covenant, I and thou; and let it be for a witness between me and thee. And Jacob took a stone, and set it up for a pillar." Genesis 31:44-46

"Also I heard the voice of the Lord, saying, Whom shall I send, and who will go for us? Then said I, Here am I; send me." Isaiah 6:8

All The Day Long

All the day long I will praise God and follow his guidance. I will love, trust and obey His word. I will call upon the name of the Lord in good times and bad times. I will bathe in and feed on His word daily. I know that there is no life outside of God. All the day long he preserves me and keeps me. He is my shelter and my shield. He allows me to be here. It is time for me to put him first all the day long.

"In God we boast all the day long, and praise thy name for ever. Selah." Psalm 44:8

Study

Study the word and live the word. God is so good to us each and every day. He has given us hope, direction, guidance, and salvation through his son Jesus. We must study and seek the word of God daily moving in the directions of life. Help us, Lord, to know your path and not be deceived by foolish things. Help us, Lord, to study with our eyes, heart, mind, and soul open to receive the spirit of God with each study. Thank you, God, for Jesus; I know that I would have no way to you if it was not for your love. I thank you, God, for the word to study and to know what your will is for my life. Study of your word will make me stronger, increase my wisdom, develop humility, and create a new heart in me. I must continue to study.

"And that ye study to be quiet, and to do your own business, and to work with your own hands, as we commanded you;.. ."
1 Thessalonians 4:11

Trust

Help me to trust and obey. Your word and your love are my lamp and my life. Help me, God, to speak the truth to all men. Help me to demonstrate trust by my daily living. Let me trust in blissful times, sad times, hard times, and peaceful times. Help me to know that trust is neither anxious nor fearful. To trust we must become vulnerable; we must be willing to accept that we do not know everything, nor are we in control of anything. Trust is being dependent on your word to lead my life. Trusting in You, Lord, is my blessing.

"Trust in the LORD with all thine heart; and lean not unto thine own understanding. In all thy ways acknowledge him, and he shall direct thy paths." Proverbs 3:5-6

"He trusted in the LORD God of Israel; so that after him was none like him among all the kings of Judah, nor any that were before him." 2 Kings 18:5

We Can Do It Through Christ

We can, we can, and we can! Through Christ we can do all things. We can be a strong soldier, a valiant warrior in the Lord. We can go on when it seems difficult to move forward. We can love the Lord by loving His people daily. We can spread joy as we move from place to place. The things we can do through Christ are not selfish things, but things that are representative of Christ. It is not about us achieving self-centered ambitions to outdo others. It is through the concern for our fellow man and obedience to his word that we can succeed. We can show love, kindness, and patience to others as we live. Each of us has something that we are dealing with. Be kinder than you think you need to be. Be forgiving when you are violated. Be merciful when someone has dealt with you harshly. You may be the example of Christ for those in need.

"Not that I speak in respect of want: for I have learned, in whatsoever state I am, therewith to be content. I know both how to be abased, and I know how to abound: every where and in all things I am instructed both to be full and to be hungry, both to abound and to suffer need. I can do all things through Christ which strengtheneth me." Philippians 4:11-14

God is So Good

I thank you, God, for being so good to me. I thank
you for being so good to my family, friends, and
people we pray for and interact with each day.
God, I thank you for loving me so much. Thank
you for providing me opportunities to grow and
become a better person. I am thankful to you, God,
for growing me to see how my challenges and
joys all lead me to ways of becoming the person
you know I need to be. Thank you for spending
so much time with me. Thank you for hearing my
prayers. Thank you for teaching me to bring all
things both large and small to you. Thank you
for your patience with me. Thank you for turning
me in the right direction. My God is so good.

"And when he was gone forth into the way, there came one running,
and kneeled to him, and asked him, Good Master, what shall I do that I
may inherit eternal life? And Jesus said unto him, Why callest thou me
good? There is none good but one, that is, God." Mark 10:17-18

God Is So Real

God is so real in my life and he keeps his promises. God gave us his son. I thank God for sparing my life and bringing me hope. I recognize that I am nothing without God. There are so many things that I am not aware of and he protects me from them each day. God takes care of so many of my needs without my asking him. There are times when I am not conscious that I need God to rescue me. God is so real in my life. You have worked wonders in my life. God, I cannot imagine the strength, power, and love it took for you to give your son to die for sinners. Thank you for showing us our value to you and adopting us through the blood of Christ.

"According as he hath chosen us in him before the foundation of the world, that we should be holy and without blame before him in love: Having predestinated us unto the adoption of children by Jesus Christ to himself, according to the good pleasure of his will . . ." Ephesians 1:4-5

Blessings

Blessings fall like rain. We cannot count all
the blessing we receive each day. We receive
blessings from all directions. Blessings shine like
the sun's rays. The rays of blessings brighten and
transform our lives. Blessings flow like rivers of
water bringing peace and serenity in our lives.
Blessings give us life's breaths each moment to live.
Blessings surround us as air. We are enveloped in
an enclosure of protection and grace. Be grateful
for your blessings, thank God who provides
generously. Have you been a blessing today? It is
important that we are liberal with our blessings.

"Even by the God of thy father, who shall help thee; and by the Almighty,
who shall bless thee with blessings of heaven above, blessings of the
deep that lieth under, blessings of the breasts, and of the womb:"
Genesis 49:25

Lord Help Me To Breathe

Lord, help me as the thoughts in my mind run so rapidly. Lord, help me as I try and process the many things in my life to know that you are providing me opportunities. Lord, help me to breathe as I move in another direction. Lord, help me as I examine myself daily and probe deeper and deeper within myself to mine the gold that is within me according to your word. Lord, help me when I feel overwhelmed by the pressures of this world. Lord, help me to breathe you in and exhale the worries and problems of today. Lord, help me to celebrate your love and joy you give me each day. Lord, thank you for giving me this breath.

"And the LORD God formed man of the dust of the ground, and breathed into his nostrils the breath of life; and man became a living soul." Genesis 2:7

Each Day Is A New Opportunity

How do you start your day? When do you start your day? Do you start to think about your day upon waking in the morning, or do you start to think about it as you're going to sleep? If you are about to start a new enterprise, for example, a new job, new marriage, new location, new child in your life; when do you begin planning for your first day? When do you seek God? Is it before you start, after or not at all? Do you look to the world and its logic to make your decisions or wait on God for your answers? Have you received the response you were looking for from the world? Who is reliable, the world or God?

"But seek ye first the kingdom of God, and his righteousness; and all these things shall be added unto you. Take therefore no thought for the morrow: for the morrow shall take thought for the things of itself. Sufficient unto the day is the evil thereof." Matthew 6:33-34

What Is Your Fuel

What kind of attitude and thoughts do you bring to your mind each day? Is it an attitude of enthusiasm? Your attitude can work positively or negatively. Your thoughts can allow you to make great leaps forward toward opportunities. Your thoughts can also work to keep you from taking that first step away from the fears and apprehensions that you harbor, or the beliefs that have held you in the fearful closet of your negative thoughts. We are powerful beings, possessing many God-given abilities. Put on the mind of God and be a better person. Use what God has given you to be a blessing to and for others. After all, we are made in God's image. There is no better image in the world.

"So God created man in his own image, in the image of God created he him; male and female created he them." Genesis 1:27.

"Let this mind be in you, which was also in Christ Jesus: Who, being in the form of God, thought it not robbery to be equal with God: But made himself of no reputation, and took upon him the form of a servant, and was made in the likeness of men:.." Philippians 2:5-7

"For I know the thoughts that I think toward you, saith the Lord, thoughts of peace, and not of evil, to give you an expected end." Jeremiah 29:11

Opportunities For Good

We can create opportunity for good. Are you creating good opportunities? Do you recognize opportunity? Are you recognizing your opportunities to do good? Simply by living, we are granted a new opportunity to be creative in helping others. By having a positive attitude, by emptying our minds of negativity and fear, we can see pathways that fear and negativity can block us from seeing. By intentionally seeking opportunities to serve during the course of the day, we will find them. What we do in small and big ways count when we do it with no expectation of reciprocity.

"And let us not be weary in well doing: for in due season we shall reap, if we faint not. As we have therefore opportunity, let us do good unto all men, especially unto them who are of the household of faith." Galatians 6:9-10

Only Fear The Lord

The fear of the world will trap us and immobilize us. It will spin us out of control and toss us to and fro and create negative thoughts. Clear your mind of all negativity and fear. Use a truthful conscience and pray to do all things that are good. Do all things the right way. Get rid of negative thoughts – they add no value. When God wakes us up, we can allow ourselves to perceive and believe the opportunities that God has for us. We have a choice. We can choose to count our blessings and use the talents, skills, and abilities he has given us to serve him in truth with all our heart. He has given all for us. Fear God and follow him.

"For the Lord will not forsake his people for his great name's sake: because it hath pleased the Lord to make you his people. Moreover as for me, God forbid that I should sin against the Lord in ceasing to pray for you: but I will teach you the good and the right way: Only fear the Lord, and serve him in truth with all your heart: for consider how great things he hath done for you."
1 Samuel 12:22-24

Blessings Are Gifts

Lord of all, shower us with your blessings. You give us blessings abundantly and without ceasing. The Lord is blessing us right now in so many ways. He continues to bless us as he grants us life each day. Thank God for allowing you to rise with each new day. Thank God for the breath he gives you all along the way. God blessed us with the greatest gift of all, his son. Have you ever received such a gift before? Do you realize your worth? God gave you His blessing. Accept the gifts.

"Every good gift and every perfect gift is from above, and cometh down from the Father of lights, with whom is no variableness, neither shadow of turning." James 1:17

"As every man hath received the gift, even so minister the same one to another, as good stewards of the manifold grace of God." 1 Peter 4:10

Follow

I will follow the Lord. I am blessed by him each day
of my life. I will enjoy the blessings he gives me. I
will always follow God. He is my creator. I did not
create myself or anything in this world. I will follow
God's directions and be his blessing here on earth.
I will go where God sends me and stop when he
directs me. I have learned to surrender to God.
I will not be led by the world or the things of the
world. I have learned to follow God. I will follow him
all the way, all the day, and with him I will stay.

"Then said Jesus unto his disciples, If any man will come after me, let
him deny himself, and take up his cross, and follow me." Matthew 16:24

I Will Go On

When the days are long and the nights are
short, I will go on. When the sky is gray and the
path is unclear, I will go on. When chaos reigns
and peace seems elusive, I will go on. When
time seems to fly and things mount up, I will
go on. I will go on no matter what the day may
bring. I will not be defeated by the devil. I will
go on because I have a foundation that is sure.
I will go on because of him who lives in me.

"For he looked for a city which hath foundations, whose builder and
maker is God." Hebrews 11:10

"Nevertheless the foundation of God standeth sure, having this seal,
The Lord knoweth them that are his. And, let every one that nameth
the name of Christ depart from iniquity." 2 Timothy 2:19

Delivered

Sometimes life seems heavy. Sometimes life seems to pull and tug on your entire being. Sometimes it feels hard, like life is trying to crush you. Sometimes it appears that life has it in for you. But don't give up, because God can make a way for you. God can deliver you. Don't give in, because God is available to you. Put your faith, your trust, your obedience in God; no matter what comes your way, you can grow stronger. You can be delivered by God if you keep His word. So, be tired, but keep going – be of God.

"And Deborah said unto Barak, Up; for this is the day in which the LORD hath delivered Sisera into thine hand: is not the LORD gone out before thee? So Barak went down from mount Tabor, and ten thousand men after him." Judges 4:14

Priorities

Lord, I want to do the right thing. I want to do things right. I want to have the right mind. I want to have the right heart. I want to focus on the right things. I want to live the right life. Lord, I want to be of service and be thankful to do your good works. I want to have the right attitude as I serve here on earth. I want to be in the right places and place myself rightly. Lord, help me to keep your word so that I will have my priorities right. Let me always seek you first in all things. Lord, let me make your priorities my priorities.

"And Jesus answered him, The first of all the commandments is, Hear, O Israel; The Lord our God is one Lord: And thou shalt love the Lord thy God with all thy heart, and with all thy soul, and with all thy mind, and with all thy strength: this is the first commandment. And the second is like, namely this, Thou shalt love thy neighbour as thyself. There is none other commandment greater than these. " Mark 12:29-31

In A Better Land

When I no longer walk the mortal life, I shall see without eyes. My understanding will be fully developed, and my consciousness will be present with the Lord. I will understand that God will have the full perspective on each of our lives. We will give an account for what we did and did not do while on earth. I will be able to talk with God and rest in Him. The choice to follow God will have already been made. I will interface with God in a full manner of awareness. I will sing his praise and convey my love day by day. I look forward to no tears, no pain, and no sorrows, where peace and love are the way of life. I want to see the lamb and lion walking together and joy being shared. In a better land, we will walk golden streets and people will desire to worship God constantly. I want to live in a better land.

"And God shall wipe away all tears from their eyes; and there shall be no more death, neither sorrow, nor crying, neither shall there be any more pain: for the former things are passed away." Revelation 21:4

The Longer

The longer you pray, the longer you will stay
close to the Lord. The longer you give, the more
you will want to give and the more will be given
to you. The longer you are merciful to others,
the more mercy will be shown to you. The longer
you provide comfort to those in need, the more
comfort you will receive in your time of need. Be
more than you think you can be for God. Be patient
with yourself in the Lord. The longer you stay with
God, the more of his beauty will be seen in you.
Shine, Jesus, shine through and in my life today.

"Who is among you that feareth the LORD, that obeyeth the voice of
his servant, that walketh in darkness, and hath no light? Let him trust in
the name of the LORD, and stay upon his God." Isaiah 50:10

Believe It

I believe it because I know that there are things
that I can't explain that have brought joy to my
life. There are things that defy all understanding,
yet they happen. There are things that surprise
us despite the track record of past issues. There
are things that cannot be accounted for by man.
Believe it, pray about it, and achieve it through
Christ. Know that God is working in your life for
your good. Sometimes our blessings are found in
the worst things or the problems of life. Learn to
trust in God, not in what you can see for yourself.

"For this cause also thank we God without ceasing, because, when ye
received the word of God which ye heard of us, ye received it not as
the word of men, but as it is in truth, the word of God, which effectually
worketh also in you that believe." 1 Thessalonians 2:13

Let Me Walk

Let me walk with you while I travel through this life. Let me know that you are near and will always be there for me. Let me see that the world has no fears that can amount to anything in comparison to you. Let me feel the warmth of your care, the gentleness of your spirit, and the brightness of your love. Dear Lord, let me walk the walk with you today, tomorrow, and always. Let me be your child for life. The only name I will use is Christian as I follow Christ.

"But take diligent heed to do the commandment and the law, which Moses the servant of the LORD charged you, to love the LORD your God, and to walk in all his ways, and to keep his commandments, and to cleave unto him, and to serve him with all your heart and with all your soul." Joshua 22:5

Love Is

Love is taking the time to express one's feelings
of joy, elation, and adoration to those around
us today. Love is knowing that we have a safe,
secure haven of rest in God everyday. Love is
going forward and doing good, even when it seems
going forward is hard to do. Love is counting the
good things in life and the blessings we receive
so abundantly and giving thanks. Love is not
discounting the peace, joy, and happiness of each
day. Love is smiling and giving hope because you
can. Love is powerful, it changes things. Love is
a gift of God, take time to love. Be lovable, give
love, accept love, and know that God is love.

"Beloved, let us love one another: for love is of God; and every one that
loveth is born of God, and knoweth God. He that loveth not knoweth
not God; for God is love." 1 John 4:7-8

I Need You Lord

Dear Lord, help me, please, with myself. Help me to know that you are with me through all my trials, tribulations, fears, anguish and pain. Dear Lord, I need you to guide me when I think I am strong, guide me when I think I know it all, guide me when I know I need your direction. Please, Lord, just guide me. I need you, Lord, more than I know and understand. I need you, Lord, through my moments of anger, through my feelings of weakness, and when I want to speak without love. I need you, Lord, as my hope and my dreams. I want my happiness to be based in your love. Teach me, Lord, to depend on you to fulfill my needs.

"Let all those that seek thee rejoice and be glad in thee: let such as love thy salvation say continually, The LORD be magnified. But I am poor and needy; yet the Lord thinketh upon me: thou art my help and my deliverer; make no tarrying, O my God." Psalm 40:16-17

I Will Praise Him

I will trust in him who will not leave me. I will hold to his unchanging hands. I will love Jesus and follow him all the way. I will praise the name of Jesus because he is worthy to be praised. I will call on the name of Jesus because he always answers. Jesus is the greatest name I know. Yes, I love Jesus because he has done so much for me. I will give glory to God daily and ask for strength to glorify him in all that I do.

"The LORD is my strength and my shield; my heart trusted in him, and I am helped: therefore my heart greatly rejoiceth; and with my song will I praise him." Psalm 28:7

God Is So Good

God is so good to me and you each day. He is
so good we need to repeat the phrase each day.
He leads my life for my good and to better me
each day. God is ever present in my life. God is
so good; he allows me to move as my knowledge
and faith grow in him. God is so good; he is patient
with me as I take small steps in the faith. God is
so good and I am so thankful that he cares so
much for me and you. Why don't you trust God
today and allow his goodness to bless your life?

"I will extol thee, my God, O king; and I will bless thy name for ever and
ever. Every day will I bless thee; and I will praise thy name for ever and
ever. Great is the LORD, and greatly to be praised; and his greatness is
unsearchable. One generation shall praise thy works to another, and
shall declare thy mighty acts." Psalm 145:1-4

Taking Care

Thank you for taking care of me and my household. Help me to be the one that helps others here on this earth for your name's sake. Help me to know that I have a responsibility to you to take care of others. Grow my understanding in your ways for my talents, abilities, and skills. Let me use what you have given me to glorify you today. Lord, help me to serve you with thanksgiving as I am serving others. God, I thank you for the opportunities to serve. Let your love, your peace, and your spirit be seen in me in the small things and the big things. I thank you for taking care of me. Thank you for delivering me from myself and my enemies. Lord, you are always taking care of me and I know your love never fails.

"And went to him, and bound up his wounds, pouring in oil and wine, and set him on his own beast, and brought him to an inn, and took care of him. And on the morrow when he departed, he took out two pence, and gave them to the host, and said unto him, Take care of him; and whatsoever thou spendest more, when I come again, I will repay thee. Which now of these three, thinkest thou, was neighbour unto him that fell among the thieves? And he said, He that shewed mercy on him. Then said Jesus unto him, Go, and do thou likewise." Luke 10:34-37

I Want To Thank You

I want to thank you for not giving up on me. I want to thank you for seeing the good in me. I want to thank you for bringing me this far. I want to thank you for allowing me to grow beyond my level of ease. I want to thank you for seeing what I can be through your sculpting me into a very fine and valuable creation. Thank you for seeing the worth in me, to die that I might live. I want to thank you for allowing me to see the changes in me and to know that it is not my doing. I want to thank you for allowing others to know that I am yours by the power, strength, and good works that you assign me to do for you. Thank you for letting me glorify you by the work you give me to do for you. Thank you for expressing your love for me and for all who will obey.

"But God be thanked, that ye were the servants of sin, but ye have obeyed from the heart that form of doctrine which was delivered you."
Romans 6:17

Lord What Do I Do

Lord, what do I do with the blessing you gave me? What do I need to understand in order to use my blessings? Lord, how am I supposed to use these blessing? Are these blessings good things that I should give away, or are they here to help me through something in the future? Lord, are they meant to bring me joy or pain? Am I to understand how pain is a reminder to enjoy the high points of life, and how much pain can indicate that it is time to make a change? Lord, what is it that you want me to do for you today to glorify your name? Should I be still? Should I make a change? Should I take the time and enjoy what I have right now? Should I move slowly from where I am now, or should I run? Decisions, decisions, Lord, I need your help with all my decisions!

"All scripture is given by inspiration of God, and is profitable for doctrine, for reproof, for correction, for instruction in righteousness: That the man of God may be perfect, thoroughly furnished unto all good works."
2 Timothy 3:15-17

To Be With God

Oh Lord, you know my heart and where I have been. You know where I came from and why I was there. Lord, you know that I love you and that I want to be a symbol of your love by my life. Lord, you know that I love you and want to be pleasing to you. Lord, I want to be with you. Help me to live a life that will honor and serve you. Lord, you know how I feel when I go through a trial in my life, and I thank you for being God. Lord, you know what it will take to get me where you want me to be. Help me, Lord, to be what you want and do to what you want. Help me as I struggle to decrease, so that you may increase in my life. Help me, Lord, to know that you find favor in me when I am obedient to your will. Lord, please help me to never disappoint you because of my selfishness. Lord, I want to be pleasing to you when I talk, walk, and think. I want to do the right thing. Please, Lord, be with me; and I want to be with you, God.

"And Jacob vowed a vow, saying, If God will be with me, and will keep me in this way that I go, and will give me bread to eat, and raiment to put on, So that I come again to my father's house in peace; then shall the LORD be my God: And this stone, which I have set for a pillar, shall be God's house: and of all that thou shalt give me I will surely give the tenth unto thee." Genesis 28:19-22

Lord Help Me To Make It

Dear Lord, my life feels heavy and so overwhelming. It seems that there is so much to do and so much that needs to be done. Dear Lord, help me to focus on the right things. Help me to move and grow in the direction of your love and grace. Dear Lord, I need your strength to hold on to right now. Lord, never leave me alone. I cannot make it on my own. Lord, help me to make it one day at a time. Lord, help me to make it as I walk by faith and not by sight. Lord, help me to make it when I am weak at heart. Lord, I put my trust in you to help me to make it.

"They part my garments among them, and cast lots upon my vesture. But be not thou far from me, O LORD: O my strength, haste thee to help me." Psalm 22:18-19

Lord You Know

Lord, you know who we are and who we can be. Lord, you know things about us that we may never know. Lord, we need you to direct our lives in every way. Lord, you know we are not able to help ourselves from ourselves. Lord, help us to know that we are not the masters of our lives. Lord, lead us in ways that will help us and others. Lord, you know when we are going in the wrong direction as we often do with our minds made up to do what we want to do. Help us, Lord, to stop and seek your guidance in our lives daily. Help us to want to serve you. Open our hearts to know that you know us from the inside out, and that we work best when we follow your will for our lives.

"There is none holy as the LORD: for there is none beside thee: neither is there any rock like our God. Talk no more so exceeding proudly; let not arrogancy come out of your mouth: for the LORD is a God of knowledge, and by him actions are weighed. The bows of the mighty men are broken, and they that stumbled are girded with strength."
1 Samuel 2:2-4

Let's Talk

Hello, how are you? Are you feeling well? How is your spirit? Are you okay with how you are today? How are you getting along in life? How are you, really? How are you in the heat of the moment? How are you in dark places? How are you when people are yelling at you? How are you when things are going well? How are you internally? Are you calm or screaming? Are you fearful or courageous? Are you looking for the next thing or are you content in all situations? Are you filled with the truth or lies? Are you part of the darkness or light? Are you full of doubt or faith? Let's talk about how you are.

"The LORD made not this covenant with our fathers, but with us, even us, who are all of us here alive this day. The LORD talked with you face to face in the mount out of the midst of the fire . . ." Deuteronomy 5:3-4

"And ye said, Behold, the LORD our God hath showed us his glory and his greatness, and we have heard his voice out of the midst of the fire: we have seen this day that God doth talk with man, and he liveth." Deuteronomy 5:24

Thank You

I am thankful that you are my father who loves and cares for me. I know that you know me best and what is best for me. You will always lead me to the path of righteousness and love for my fellow man. I trust that you will provide and give us the things we need, because you created us. I pray, Lord, that you give us the strength to go on in your word regardless of the mountains in our path. Lord, bless us and keep us strong in your ways. Help us to help ourselves and build on the blessings you give us continually. Lord, let me see you in everything I do. Lord, bless our relationship to grow in my commitment to you. Lord, help me to surrender my will to yours. I want to thank you, Lord, for being present in my life.

"In every thing give thanks: for this is the will of God in Christ Jesus concerning you." 1 Thessalonians 5:18

I Will Call

I will call upon the Lord who will always be available to me. I will live according to God's word because in it are the words that give life. I will listen for your quiet voice early in the morning. I will embrace your peace, for there is no other peace that can surpass all understanding. I will sing unto you, Lord, because singing makes my heart joyful to praise you with the voice you gave me. I will call upon you, Lord, because you keep your promises.

"The God of my rock; in him will I trust: he is my shield, and the horn of my salvation, my high tower, and my refuge, my saviour; thou savest me from violence. I will call on the Lord, who is worthy to be praised: so shall I be saved from mine enemies." II Samuel 22:3-4

Do You Believe

Do you believe in what you can't see? Believe in all things you know are from God. Believe without wavering. Trust that God will lead rightly. Do you believe in your job, money, things, and personhood? What do you think you have created? What kind of patience do you show? What are your thoughts about? What do you do when someone does you wrong? Where is the life you gave for others? Do you believe you are able to do everything on your own? I implore you not to think highly of yourself, but of God for all he has done for us.

"Who verily was foreordained before the foundation of the world, but was manifest in these last times for you, Who by him do believe in God, that raised him up from the dead, and gave him glory; that your faith and hope might be in God. Seeing ye have purified your souls in obeying the truth through the Spirit unto unfeigned love of the brethren, see that ye love one another with a pure heart fervently:" 1 Peter 1:20-22

Praise God

Praise God and trust Him in all things. Let God rule your life and give Him the glory. Trust that we only know in part, but God knows the whole of our lives. Help us, Lord, to live with ourselves. We need to get to know ourselves, and to know that we need to examine our lives daily. Lord, when the darkest time comes, the enemy attacks; when life gets difficult, when the storms of life inflict pains above that which we think we can handle, let us praise God. We praise you, God, for all things. We praise you for overcoming the world. We praise you because you are God.

"God is gone up with a shout, the LORD with the sound of a trumpet. Sing praises to God, sing praises: sing praises unto our King, sing praises. For God is the King of all the earth: sing ye praises with understanding." Psalm 47:5-7

Lord Give Me Strength

Lord, will you give me the strength I need to serve you? Lord, as I share your word some people frown, or move away, or say they are still having too much fun to become a Christian. There are times when some people have said foul words, or they shut the door, saying they don't want to hear that stuff. Lord, give me strength to love them anyway. Lord, give me strength to know that they are not rejecting me. Lord, give me the strength to keep trying. Lord, help me to live my life so others can see that my strength is not my own. Lord, help others to see me depending on you for my life. I know that you have taken care of me in the past and that I can rest assured that you will provide for my needs. Lord, thank you for giving me strength; help me to use it for your glory.

"The LORD will give strength unto his people; the LORD will bless his people with peace." Psalm 29:11

God The Father

My God is an awesome God. He delights my heart with joy and love. He teaches me how to hold on when I feel I am only hanging by a thread. He gives me what I need when I need it and many times before I know I need it. He graces my life with peace, love, and happiness. He blesses me beyond what I could ever think or ask for. God is good to me, and I am thankful. God gives me good gifts like no other father can. Put your faith in God so that he can be good to you, too.

"Truly God is good to Israel, even to such as are of a clean heart." Psalm 73:1

" ... And commanded Judah to seek the LORD God of their fathers, and to do the law and the commandment." 2 Chronicles 14:4

Follow Christ

The life we live is a reflection of the thoughts that are in our hearts. The way we judge or view things is based on the experiences and beliefs we have. The way we interact with others is based on how we have been treated and how we perceive the treatment of others. The way we can live fully is by living a life as a Christian following Christ who gives us life. A life in Christ is more valuable than any earthly treasure we can accumulate. Live by the example of the best: Follow Christ.

"For even hereunto were ye called: because Christ also suffered for us, leaving us an example, that ye should follow his steps:" 1 Peter 2:21

Choices

The way we feel, the way we sing, the way we love are all choices that we make. The way we hold on to some things and not others is based on the choices we make. The way we form relationships with people and the way we avoid relationships with others are reflections of the choices we make. The way we give in and the way we give up are the limitations we place on ourselves by our choices. The way we accept some things, people, places, and our own feelings is the direct result of the exposure we had and the perceptions we have formed from the experiences we had. We have a choice. We can live for this life or for eternal life. You can make the choice right now. Which is it?

"And when there had been much disputing, Peter rose up, and said unto them, Men and brethren, ye know how that a good while ago God made choice among us, that the Gentiles by my mouth should hear the word of the gospel, and believe." Acts 15:7

Lord You Know

Lord, you know what is right for me and when it is right for me. Lord, you have prepared a way for me that will serve me best as I do your will. Lord, you don't see as I see, and I am thankful for that. Lord, you have provided great things for me and you want me to see how you have prepared me to have great things and a great life. Help me to want to be used by you each day. I thank you for bringing me where I am today. Lord, you know my words and my deeds. Let me not grow weary when others try to find fault with the work I do for you. Let me give you the glory for what you allow me to do on this earth.

"For I know the thoughts that I think toward you, saith the LORD, thoughts of peace, and not of evil, to give you an expected end." Jeremiah 29:11

"And whatsoever ye do in word or deed, do all in the name of the Lord Jesus, giving thanks to God and the Father by him." Colossians 3:17

Lord Help Me

Lord, help me as I struggle with unknown enemies that try to pull me into unrighteousness. Lord, give me the capacity to hold on to you, no matter what happens in my life. Lord, give me the virtue to love even when others are mistreating me. Lord, help me to believe that everything and everyone you made are good. Help me to understand that some people have not recognized that they were created by you and they behave in the ways of a lost soul. Lord, help me to help someone see your love for them. Help me to live my life showing others that I believe that Jesus is alive today because your light shines through me.

"Be pleased, O LORD, to deliver me: O LORD, make haste to help me."
Psalm 40:13

"Then came she and worshipped him, saying, Lord, help me."
Matthew 15:25

Lord Help Me To Go On

Lord, help me to go on through the good times seeking you when I am prosperous. Lord, help me to go on seeking you when I am facing the loss of a loved one. Lord, help me to go on when I am unemployed and forlorn. Lord, help me to go on when others around me are acknowledging some good you have allowed me to do. Lord, help me to have the desire to improve for you as I live. Lord, help me not to want to emulate those who are negative and unmoving. Lord, help me to make a positive difference in the world and in the lives of those with whom I come in contact.

"Help me, O LORD my God: O save me according to thy mercy:" Psalm 109:26

"Let your conversation be without covetousness; and be content with such things as ye have: for he hath said, I will never leave thee, nor forsake thee. So that we may boldly say, The Lord is my helper, and I will not fear what man shall do unto me." Hebrews 13:5-7

Believe

I believe that life is a blessing and that we have a special opportunity to experience living. I believe that life can be a wonderful experience, no matter what situations we encounter. I believe that we can learn more about ourselves if we are willing to let go of fears, "shoulds," and "should nots" in our lives. I believe that we can stand in our own way and miss out on blessings because we have to have it our way. I believe that we can achieve much more with God in our lives than we could ever come close to without him.

"And the LORD said unto Moses, Lo, I come unto thee in a thick cloud, that the people may hear when I speak with thee, and believe thee for ever. And Moses told the words of the people unto the LORD." Exodus 19:9

"Jesus answered and said unto them, This is the work of God, that ye believe on him whom he hath sent." John 6:29

Your Way Lord

Lord, help me to live by your love which guides us in the truth. Lord, help me to be fertile ground for your word to take root and grow in me each day. Lord, help me to understand that I will not always be able to see the blessing you are giving me and others, but help me to thank you anyway. Lord, help me not to fall from your grace and become a part of the world. Lord, help me not to sin willfully. Lord, let me do things your way and with the right heart. Lord, help me to be the person you would have me to be to enter your kingdom. Lord, I know my way, my thoughts, my actions are not always in line with your word. Please forgive me; I am learning to depend more and more on you and less on myself. Thank you, God, for loving me as I learn.

"For if ye shall diligently keep all these commandments which I command you, to do them, to love the LORD your God, to walk in all his ways, and to cleave unto him; . . ." Deuteronomy 11:22

Dream

Dream and envision the possibilities. Dream and allow your mind the freedom to produce beautiful, wonderful, extraordinary pictures, places, and things. Dream and see beyond the limits and constraints you have learned from others or your own experiences. Dream and be more than you thought you wanted to be. See more than you thought you could have, be stronger than you imagined yourself being. Know that all things are possible through Christ who strengthens you, so dream of how you can serve the Lord.

"As for these four children, God gave them knowledge and skill in all learning and wisdom: and Daniel had understanding in all visions and dreams." Daniel 1:17

"And it shall come to pass in the last days, saith God, I will pour out of my Spirit upon all flesh: and your sons and your daughters shall prophesy, and your young men shall see visions, and your old men shall dream dreams:" Acts 2:16-18

Life

Life is a blessing, and we can live in a way that shows gratitude for the life we have been given. God has been good to us by giving us wonderful blessings and preparing us each day for greater things. Life is for blessing others and providing positive benefits as we pass through the stages of our path. Life is not promised to us. Life is a blessing. Give thanks. Be careful what you expect in others, because it will reveal what we might not want to see in our lives. If you look for good or bad, it shows our heart. Life will give us what we look for in others. Be willing to face what is in your heart and see what resides there. Be loving, kind, gentle, reasonable, and full of prayer.

"And the LORD God formed man of the dust of the ground, and breathed into his nostrils the breath of life; and man became a living soul." Genesis 2:7

Everlasting Life

What kind of life are you living? Are you considerate of others? Do you live for yourself only? Do you judge others by your likes and dislikes? Do you use the blessings you have been given to be a blessing? Be prayerful for each other. Yes, it does make a difference how we live and how we treat one another. Make sure the life you live is the story you want told about you. Be filled with right things so that right things will flow forth from you. Look not only on the things you need for today but the things that will bring you everlasting life. This life is not your own. You, as I, have been given a mission to accomplish here on earth for God. Do the work of him who sent you with joy. Build your treasures where it counts. Be obedient to God and serve him and receive everlasting life.

"Labour not for the meat which perisheth, but for that meat which endureth unto everlasting life, which the Son of man shall give unto you: for him hath God the Father sealed." John 6:27

The Lord

The Lord has blessed you today. What are you going to do to thank him? The Lord gives us life and so much more. The Lord saves us from ourselves daily. He fills our lives with love, hope, and joy. Do we pay attention to the great blessings, or do we focus on what we don't have, or what we didn't get? He keeps us going when things are hard. He loves us when we don't feel that anyone else does. He holds us and cares for us in ways only the savior can. I am thankful for the Lord and his presence in my life. Are you? I am thankful to the Lord for counting me worthy to serve him. I am thankful to the Lord for all his grace which I need so abundantly. The Lord is our Redeemer. Thank you, Lord, for loving us; help us to pass it on.

"And the LORD God took the man, and put him into the garden of Eden to dress it and to keep it." Genesis 2:15

"And thou shalt love the Lord thy God with all thy heart, and with all thy soul, and with all thy mind, and with all thy strength: this is the first commandment." Mark 12:30

Let It Be

Let it be for righteousness. Allow yourself to give in and surrender to the Lord. Let it be God who works wonders in your life. Let it be and free yourself of self, fear, anger, lies, hate, foolishness, and bitterness. Let your life be for God and you will see a change in your life today.

"Now therefore come thou, let us make a covenant, I and thou; and let it be for a witness between me and thee." Genesis 31:43-44

"Peace I leave with you, my peace I give unto you: not as the world giveth, give I unto you. Let not your heart be troubled, neither let it be afraid." John 14:27

Lord Clean Me

Dear Lord, I come to you in prayer asking your peace, love, and mercy in my life. Dear Lord, my heart is heavy and afraid. Lord, it seems my path is crisscrossed with craters and mountains. Lord, help me to go on in spite of the barriers that are before me. Lord, help me to believe and trust that you will always be there for me. Dear Lord, I need you to clean me up. Lord, I don't want to be taken in by evil or darkness. Lord, I know I need you to help my heart release the things of the world. Lord, I want to have a pure heart. I want to be a sanctuary for you. Lord, empty me of me; Lord, clean me of me.

"Therefore the LORD hath recompensed me according to my righteousness; according to my cleanness in his eye sight." 2 Samuel 22:25

"And, behold, there came a leper and worshipped him, saying, Lord, if thou wilt, thou canst make me clean." Matthew 8:2

Surrender

Lord, help me to surrender my life to you. I am struggling with unknown forces. I am battling with a powerful source. Lord, I don't know who or what my challenger is, but it feels strong, as though I am in the lion's den as Daniel. Sometimes, Lord, I feel smothered, like Jonah in the belly of the whale; or even like the Hebrew children in the fiery furnace. No matter what I feel, I know that you will deliver me if I hold on to your word and have faith in God. I know this struggle can be for my betterment. I don't understand where and how it will be a blessing for me, but I know it will. For you have told me to count it all joy when I fall into diverse temptations in my life. You have also told me to thank God for all things. So, no matter what I go through in this life, I know you will never leave me nor forsake me. I know that you are working in my life so that I can be more like Christ and less like me. Thank you, God, for helping me to surrender to you.

"My brethren, count it all joy when ye fall into divers temptations; Knowing this, that the trying of your faith worketh patience. But let patience have her perfect work, that ye may be perfect and entire, wanting nothing." James 1:2-4

"Giving thanks always for all things unto God and the Father in the name of our Lord Jesus Christ; . . ." Ephesians 5:20

God Will Take Care of You

God, I thank you for bringing me through my
past of walking disorderly toward your word.
Help me to continue to hold fast to what is right
and just. You have delivered me from evil things
and people that I didn't even know were trying
to destroy me. You have taught me to seek out
righteousness, purity, and the virtues of God. You
have taught me to celebrate life and be happy
and content where I am today. God, I know you
have taken very good care of me. Thank you for
giving me another day to serve you. I know that
you are creating a better me through your love.
God will take care of you, too.

"Humble yourselves therefore under the mighty hand of God, that he
may exalt you in due time: Casting all your care upon him; for he careth
for you." 1 Peter 5:6-7

Bring

Dear Lord, I know that you are bringing me through something right now that I need to experience so that I can become a stronger soldier for you. Dear Lord, I know that you are holding my hand through whatever happens to me in my life, this world, and this generation. Dear Lord, help me in ways, which I don't know that I need help. Help me, dear Lord, to cling to you and know that you will never leave me alone or take me beyond what I can handle. You know my limits and you know my potential. Use me, Lord, especially through my pain.

"Therefore judge nothing before the time, until the Lord come, who both will bring to light the hidden things of darkness, and will make manifest the counsels of the hearts: and then shall every man have praise of God." 1 Corinthians 4:5

Be A Friend

I will be a child of God each day and live my life
in a way to stand for God. Whether there is light
or dark, I want to make sure to leave the Christian
mark. I will try to find good in everyone I meet. I
will look for opportunities to do good each day,
to be thankful, and to be available as a friend to
others. Help me to know that a friend loves at all
times. Let me be the friend who is a good listener,
a strong shoulder, and who is understanding.
Help me to let my friends know when they are
going in the wrong and right directions. Let me
be the friend who points others to Christ.

"He that hath the bride is the bridegroom: but the friend of the
bridegroom, which standeth and heareth him, rejoiceth greatly because
of the bridegroom's voice: this my joy therefore is fulfilled." John 3:29

To Be Afraid

Being afraid will take away our freedom to be joyful, happy, creative, and peaceful. Fear will steal your life a little at a time and you will reach the end of life a pauper. Fear will consume you and rule your life. Fear will keep you from living your life. Fear will keep you from knowing yourself and trusting others. Fear will take control if you let it. Free yourself, let go of fear, and trust in God. You are not in control. You are not your maker. God, your creator, cares for you. God has a plan for your life. Trust in him who will not leave you. Do not be afraid of this world or those that dwell in this world. God is in control.

"Peace I leave with you, my peace I give unto you: not as the world giveth, give I unto you. Let not your heart be troubled, neither let it be afraid." John 14:27

Let Me Come

Dear Lord, let me come to you in prayer and gladness. Let me open my eyes through my heart and know that you are my God. God, I know that you are the potter and I am the clay. You have shaped and molded me for a particular purpose. I am who I am because you have a special mission for me. Dear Lord, let me come to you with full intentions to be obedient to your will for my life. Let me display your love through my actions, choices, outreach, and personality. Help me to come to you and not be a victim in life. Let me come to you and be filled with courage from the faith that you have allowed to grow in me. Dear Lord, help me to be more like you each day. Let me come to you.

"Let my cry come near before thee, O LORD: give me understanding according to thy word." Psalm 119:169

Strength To Go On

I want to thank you, Lord, for loving me and giving me the strength to go on. Thank you, Lord, for seeing in me what I don't see in myself. Thank you, Lord, for helping me reflect on how you have saved me from myself many times. Thank you for giving me the strength to go on when I feel that I can't breathe. Yes, God, I thank you for giving me your Holy Spirit to help me, to comfort me, and to guide me in the path of righteousness. God, you have given me the strength to go on and stay focused on your word as I faced trials and tribulations. Thank you, Lord, for allowing me to step outside of myself and surrender to your will for me. Thank you for giving me the strength to go on this day.

"The LORD God is my strength, and he will make my feet like hinds' feet, and he will make me to walk upon mine high places. To the chief singer on my stringed instruments." Habakkuk 3:19

Believe

How are you living? What makes you tick?
On what are you placing your hopes, dreams,
desires, love, and life? When are you going to do
what you need to do to make the contributions
in life that are marked for you only? What do
you believe? Who do you believe in? The
world is not your friend. Your friends cannot
give you eternal life. Let your heart, life, and
power be guided by the greatest guide of all.

"When he shall come to be glorified in his saints, and to be admired in all them that believe (because our testimony among you was believed) in that day."
2 Thessalonians 1:10

Wake Up!

Wake up! This is the day that the Lord has made.
Stand up and rejoice. Live now, live where you
are, and live fully. This is the time to be counted
and counted on for being the special creation
God has made. Be courageous and experience
life in ways that you have never allowed yourself
to enjoy. Forgive, be patient, be full of love,
and allow yourself to be loved. Breathe deeply;
breathe often, filling your lungs with God's life-
giving breath. Breathe each new breath knowing
that God has given you a fresh start. Wake
up and learn of God; be of God this day.

"The Lord GOD hath given me the tongue of the learned, that I should
know how to speak a word in season to him that is weary: he wakeneth
morning by morning, he wakeneth mine ear to hear as the learned."
Isaiah 50:4

Opportunity

This is your life. You get to choose right or wrong and good or bad. You were made for a purpose. You have been given an opportunity to live for the Lord. You're a special chosen one who has a special mission in this life for this world we live in. This world would not be the way it is today without your presence. Whether you do good or bad, your actions have rippling consequences in this world. You can choose what you do with your life. Are you going to be a contributor or a taker from this world you are living in? What will you choose and when will you choose your course of action? You have many opportunities to be a positive force for God. What are you doing?

"For they that say such things declare plainly that they seek a country. And truly, if they had been mindful of that country from whence they came out, they might have had opportunity to have returned. But now they desire a better country, that is, an heavenly: wherefore God is not ashamed to be called their God: for he hath prepared for them a city." Hebrews 11:14-16

Who Are You

Who are you? Do you really know yourself and what motivates you? Do you know how you are when you are happy, sad, or angry? Would you recognize yourself if someone were to press replay on one moment in your life? Can you say that you are in a specific place in your life? Can you say with all assurance that you will do this or that and it happens? Can you say you will behave with love or hate, and, when the situation occurs, you don't recognize yourself? What can you say? If you don't know, pray about it. If you don't like what you see in yourself, pray about it. If you are willing to be transformed, renew your mind with the word of God.

"And be not conformed to this world: but be ye transformed by the renewing of your mind, that ye may prove what is that good, and acceptable, and perfect, will of God." Romans 12:2

Ask God

Ask God to lead your life, your steps, and your mind. Ask God for help each day. The Bible teaches us in John 11:22 to ask, "But I know, that even now, whatsoever thou wilt ask of God, God will give it thee." Build your hope and faith on God. Move toward letting God's word teach you how you should live and how to be godly here on earth. God can work in, through, and with your life. God is faithful. You can live an illusion or live truly. Give the control to God. He will not fail you nor forsake you. Are you ready to ask God?

"If any of you lack wisdom, let him ask of God, that giveth to all men liberally, and upbraideth not; and it shall be given him." James 1:5

Hold On

Hold on and believe. Hold on no matter how hard it gets. Hold on no matter who hurts you. Hold on no matter the expense you have. Hold on when your family or friends reject you. Hold on when you have no money and many problems. The storms may be many. Life's struggles may seem to be never ending; hold on. Through the pain, through the rain and the storms comes a more refined you. You will develop a new perspective. If you hold on and have faith in God, you will grow and become a stronger person. You can learn how to reprioritize your life in a more effective way. Trust God and you will see that, if you hold on to him, all will work out for good.

"Fight the good fight of faith, lay hold on eternal life, whereunto thou art also called, and hast professed a good profession before many witnesses."
1 Timothy 6:12

See Myself

When I see myself, life seems whole. I don't see
the challenges, the misperceptions, the weakness,
and the roughness of the road in front of me. I
see strength, faith, and forward motion. I see
love, joy, fortitude, and possibilities. Lord, help
me to see myself as you see me. Lord, help me
to live my life as a reflection of you. Lord, help
me to think as you would have me to. Help me
to see myself being obedient to your word.

"When thou goest out to battle against thine enemies,
and seest horses, and chariots, and a people more than
thou, be not afraid of them: for the LORD thy God is with
thee, which brought thee up out of the land of Egypt."
Deuteronomy 20:1

"If ye be willing and obedient, ye shall eat the good of the land:"
Isaiah 1:19

Let His Mind

Lord, let my mind be filled with things that will profit me and others. Lord, when will I become more like you and less like me? Lord, when will I surrender all to you? When will I release the clutter of my mind? When will I stop being susceptible to the junk of this world? When will I learn to live in peace, love, and joy no matter what my circumstances may be? Let me be willing to let it all go – leaving self behind and putting on the spirit of God, never looking back.

"Look not every man on his own things, but every man also on the things of others. Let this mind be in you, which was also in Christ Jesus: . . ."
Philippians 2:4-5

Teach Me

Teach me to give. Teach me to give of myself to God first. Teach me to receive nourishment of your word to myself so that I will be able to feed others. Help me to learn that, by my giving, I grow. I grow in love, grace, maturity, and in the knowledge of your will for my life. Teach me that my life matters in ways that I have not considered or imagined. Help me to desire learning and opportunities to experience what will strengthen my dependencies on you. Teach me to want more of your word in me.

"Teach me, and I will hold my tongue: and cause me to understand wherein I have erred." Job 6:24

Let Me Learn

Let me learn to be quiet. Let me learn to be quick to study your word for answers in my life. Let me learn to be patient, true, and humble with the spirit of God dwelling in me richly. God, you have blessed me for so long, you have blessed me with so much, and you have blessed me so fully. Let me learn to take each day as you give it to me, thanking you over and over again. Let me learn to thank you in the hard times and good times. Let me learn that my knowledge is limited. Let me learn that, the more I think I know, the more I need to learn. Let me continue to have a desire to learn more of you each day.

"Thy hands have made me and fashioned me: give me understanding, that I may learn thy commandments." Psalm 119:73

I Thank You

Words cannot express the love and thankfulness
I feel for you and what you have done in my life. I
will love, trust, and lean on you for all things. Help
me as I take each step to keep my eyes on you.
You have brought me through so much and I thank
you. You have cleared the way for me so many
times and I thank you. You continue to bless me
in spite of my getting in my own way. I thank you
for your faithfulness in keeping your promises. You
are the same as you were yesterday, today, and
ever will be. I can depend on you and I thank you.

"I thank my God always on your behalf, for the grace of God which is
given you by Jesus Christ; . . ." 1 Corinthians 1:4

The Creator

My Lord, direct my steps as I enter into each new day. My Lord, guide my tongue with encouraging words to say. My Lord, give my mind the peace, understanding, and wisdom to pray. My Lord, let me follow as you lead me all the way. My Lord, as I come to you, let me not hold on to the world but give it all to you before I rest. Yes, Lord, I know that you are the potter, and I am the clay. Thank you again for this day.

"Hath not the potter power over the clay, of the same lump to make one vessel unto honour, and another unto dishonour?" Romans 9:21

Bring Me Closer

Bring me closer to you, Lord. Help me to hold my head up for you. Help me to serve you with gladness in my heart and spirit. Help me to forgive and be forgiven of trespasses. Lord, bring me closer to you in small and large ways. Lord, give me strength to walk through the belly of the whale and grow in my resolve to serve you. Lord, please bring me closer to you this day.

"A man that hath friends must shew himself friendly: and there is a friend that sticketh closer than a brother." Proverbs 18:24

Let Me Pray

When my heart is heavy and the world seems full of despair, let me pray. Let me want to please you. Let me plant the seed of your word in the hearts of others. Let me look for ways to grow closer to you. Let me accept the good times and the pain in a godly way. Let me be your peace maker. Let me be used by you as you desire. Let me pray and know that you will lead the way.

"Now therefore come, let me, I pray thee, give thee counsel, that thou mayest save thine own life, and the life of thy son Solomon." 1 Kings 1:12

Are You Living Your Best Life

Are you a person of value? Do you value yourself daily? What are you doing today that is blocking your success? When you get up in the morning, do you think, I got up to go to work? When you go to your closet do you say, I wish I had better clothes? When you see your family members, do you say, what do they want from me now? So often we walk through life as if we are just taking up space and time. We see tasks and challenges as burden. Do you greet the people you see each day? Do you look around you and say, it's the same old same old? Do you feel like life is just dragging on? When you look in the mirror, do you see all the things that are wrong, you are too tall, too heavy, too fat, not enough hair? Take a moment and remember who made you.

"And the LORD God formed man of the dust of the ground, and breathed into his nostrils the breath of life; and man became a living soul." Genesis 2:7

A Better Life

I have something to share with you. You are
a person of value, a person who possesses
unfathomable abilities, talents, skills, and blessings.
Psalm 139:14 says, "I will praise you, for I am
fearfully and wonderfully made . . ." You have the
power to choose whether you want to live a life
of survival or a life of abundant living. Are you
willing to become more of who you are meant to
be? What do you want out of life? What are you
willing to give for life? If you are ready to live in
the present today, to count your blessings, to
forgive and to trust, then open your mind to this.
Each day you have is a blessing given by God.

"I am the living bread which came down from heaven: if any man eat
of this bread, he shall live for ever: and the bread that I will give is my
flesh, which I will give for the life of the world." John 6:51

Live With Joy

You have the opportunity to grow with each
challenge you face. Instead of viewing tasks as
something you have to do, view them as something
you get to do. Just think, if you changed your
perspective from "I have to feed my family" to
"I get to feed my family," you will see the joy of
having a family versus being alone. If you changed
your thoughts from "I wish I was enough" to "I
am thankful for who I am right now," you will see
how amazing you are in so many ways. Let me
go just a little farther and say, Live a life of joy.
Live with joy each day and see how blessed you
are and how much you can live your blessing.

"Then the people rejoiced, for that they offered willingly, because with
perfect heart they offered willingly to the LORD: and David the king also
rejoiced with great joy." 1 Chronicles 29:9

Bring Me Closer

Bring me close to you Lord. Help me to hold my head up. Help me to serve you with gladness of heart. Help me to forgive and be forgiven. Lord, bring me closer to you. Lord, give me strength to walk through the fiery furnace and be a brave and faithful servant for you. Lord, bring me closer to you as I worship at home, at work, at play, and while I sleep. When my heart is weary and the world seems a battlefield, bring me closer to you. Let me be the one who wants to please you with my life. Bring me closer to you, Lord, this day.

"And when the voice was past, Jesus was found alone. And they kept it close, and told no man in those days any of those things which they had they had seen." Luke 9:36

The Roads

Our life is full of color, character, and ups and downs. There are many roads we can travel and will travel: hard, convenient, and peaceful. The hard road may be filled with discomfort, hurt or despair. The convenient road may allow us to move through life quickly and feeling successful. The peaceful road can give us inner calm and consideration for the world around us. Each day may bring us a different road. How will you travel that road? Will you make the lives of others hard because your road is hard? Will you be kind when you are feeling you are on top of your game? Will you share your peace when you understand the right priorities? Get ready to travel. Each one of us will travel these roads. Travel with the grace of God.

"And when they had performed all things according to the law of the Lord, they returned into Galilee, to their own city Nazareth. And the child grew, and waxed strong in spirit, filled with wisdom: and the grace of God was upon him." Luke 2:39-40

As I Go

As I go through this land, I will open my eyes and see what God has in store for me. I know the road to heaven may be paved with many surfaces. Some surfaces may be rough like stone or gravel or with steep hills. These roads are made that way so that we can learn to handle the tough things of life. These roads will strengthen us in ways that no other roads can. Don't give up and don't run from the struggles. They will bring you to a better place in your life if you press on and face the problem. Some roads will be paved with smooth surfaces like asphalt roads and concrete sidewalks. These roads will allow us to move at a great pace and get things done with ease and little effort. They will also provide relief for a difficult road. Don't get comfortable with a smooth road; you might assume this is what life should be like all the time and come to expect only smooth sailing through life.

"And Moses said, We will go with our young and with our old, with our sons and with our daughters, with our flocks and with our herds will we go; for we must hold a feast unto the LORD. And he said unto them, Let the LORD be so with you, as I will let you go, and your little ones: look to it; for evil is before you. Not so: go now ye that are men, and serve the LORD; for that ye did desire. And they were driven out from Pharaoh's presence." Exodus 10:9-11

Are You Growing

Are you growing or are you standing still? Are you running away from life or are you facing it head on? Are you willing to take a chance and live or give up on life before you start? If we engage with the hard times and the easier times, we can grow and know who we are and how much we can take. We can seize the moments and see how well we can function in the different environments. We can choose to be distracted or we can choose to focus and stay on track. Examine yourself and see if you are going in circles or if you are growing.

"The righteous shall flourish like the palm tree: he shall grow like a cedar in Lebanon." Psalm 92:12

The Road of Peace

Will you choose the peaceful road in life? This road is paved with peace and understanding. It has gentleness, calmness, and enough to share. The waters are blue; the sky is bright with a gentle breeze. This road teaches us patience, kindness, and grace. This peace brings us a better life. The more we center ourselves in the Lord, the more we achieve in life. That achievement surpasses all understanding. The road of peace provides us the opportunities to change the world we live in. Let peace be in your inner spirit.

"Be careful for nothing; but in every thing by prayer and supplication with thanksgiving let your requests be made known unto God. And the peace of God, which passeth all understanding, shall keep your hearts and minds through Christ Jesus." Philippians 4:6-7